NO LONGER PROPERTY OF
ANYTHINK LIBRARIES/
RANGEVIEW LIBRARY DISTRICT
anythink
D0606703

Our Values

PEACE & WAR

by

Charlie Ogden

Crabtree Publishing Company
www.crabtreebooks.com
1-800-387-7650

Published in Canada
Crabtree Publishing
616 Welland Avenue
St. Catharines, ON
L2M 5V6

Published in the United States
Crabtree Publishing
PMB 59051
350 Fifth Ave, 59th Floor
New York, NY 10118

Published by Crabtree Publishing Company in 2018

First Published by Book Life in 2017
Copyright © 2017 Book Life

All rights reserved. No part of this publication may be reproduced, stored in a retrieval system or be transmitted in any form or by any means, electronic, mechanical, photocopying, recording, or otherwise, without the prior written permission of the copyright owner.

Author: Charlie Ogden

Editors: Grace Jones, Janine Deschenes

Design: Natalie Carr

Proofreader: Ellen Rodgers

Production coordinator and prepress technician (interior): Margaret Amy Salter

Prepress technician (covers): Ken Wright

Print coordinator: Margaret Amy Salter

Photographs

Shutterstock: M DOGAN p 5; Karyl Miller p 8; thomas koch p 9 (bottom right); ART production p12; punghi pp 9 (middle left), 13; pisaphotography p 17; Lucky Team Studio p 21; SpaceKris p 30 (top left); Lukasz Z p 30 (middle right); Drop of Light p 30 (bottom left)

Wikimedia: Charles Russell Collection, NARA., (front cover bottom)

All other images from Shutterstock

Printed in the USA/072017/CG20170524

Library and Archives Canada Cataloguing in Publication

Ogden, Charlie, author
Peace and war / Charlie Ogden.

(Our values)
Includes index.
Issued in print and electronic formats.
ISBN 978-0-7787-3738-4 (hardcover).--
ISBN 978-0-7787-3907-4 (softcover).--
ISBN 978-1-4271-1988-9 (HTML)

1. Peace--Juvenile literature. 2. War and society--Juvenile literature. 3. Peaceful change (International relations)--Juvenile literature. I. Title.

JZ5538.O33 2017 j303.6'6 C2017-902511-2
C2017-902512-0

Library of Congress Cataloging-in-Publication Data

Names: Ogden, Charlie, author.
Title: Peace and war / Charlie Ogden.
Description: New York, New York : Crabtree Publishing, 2018. | Series: Our values | Includes index. | Audience: Age 10-14. | Audience: Grade 4 to 6.
Identifiers: LCCN 2017016734 (print) | LCCN 2017027785 (ebook) | ISBN 9781427119889 (Electronic HTML) | ISBN 9780778737384 (reinforced library binding) | ISBN 9780778739074 (pbk.)
Subjects: LCSH: Peace--Juvenile literature. | War--Juvenile literature.
Classification: LCC JZ5538 (ebook) | LCC JZ5538 .O34 2018 (print) | DDC 303.6/6--dc23
LC record available at https://lccn.loc.gov/2017016734

CONTENTS

Words in **bold** can be found in the glossary on page 31.

PEACE AND WAR

Peace and war are two very important global **issues** today. You might see them discussed often in the media, such as on television, the Internet, and in newspapers or magazines. Peace and war are often discussed together because of their close link. War is the result of a failure to reach peace in a conflict. The terrible realities of war, and wishes for peace, are things that we often hear about every day.

"Peace" is sometimes a difficult word to define. Peace can be thought of as a state of **tranquillity**, where people are happy and everyone gets along with each other. It's often defined as the opposite of war or conflict. Some people believe that real peace isn't **sustainable**, and see peace as existing only between times of war or conflict.

"MEDIA" IS THE COLLECTIVE NAME FOR ALL OF THE POPULAR FORMS OF COMMUNICATION, SUCH AS TELEVISION, RADIO, NEWSPAPERS, AND THE INTERNET.

These symbols are known around the world as signs of peace.

War is usually described as **conflict**, violence, and fighting between separate and organized groups of people. Each side in a war will usually have their own **military**, weapons, leaders, soldiers, **tactics**, and reasons for fighting. The activities involved in fighting a war are called "warfare." And, of course, war always leads to loss of life, injured **civilians**, people being forced out of their homes, and cities and towns being destroyed.

THIS MEMORIAL IN VIRGINIA COMMEMORATES ALL U.S. MARINE CORPS WHO HAVE DIED IN BATTLE.
UNCOMMON VALOR WAS A COMMON VIRTUE

It is easy to see how living in a peaceful world would be a lot better than living in a world where wars are always being fought. Although fewer soldiers die in wars today than in almost any other period of history, many civilians are killed. There is still a long way to go before peace for all on Earth can be achieved.

Throughout history, wars have been fought for many different reasons. A prevalent cause for war has been a desire for land and resources. These include such things as land itself, food, natural resources such as water or lumber, and energy such as oil. These are the things people need to survive—and also the things that make countries wealthy and powerful. Many wars have been fought to attain power and gain land, and also to defend territory.

For almost all of human history, wars have been fought over land and resources.

It seems possible that, with our current technology, wars fought over resources could become a thing of the past. In 2015, for example, enough food was produced to feed the world's population twice over, and with today's technology we are able to transport food almost anywhere. But that food is not distributed evenly. One in every nine people—about 795 million people worldwide—still don't have enough food to eat. There is still a long way to go.

One of the most common reasons for going to war is to gain power. Civilians have gone to war against their own **governments** in order to gain power over their country. Similarly, governments have gone to war against their own people to retain, or keep, power over a country. Some leaders have gone to war because they want more power over areas of the world that have land or resources that could make them money.

Culture can also lead to war. Different groups of people around the world often experience conflict with each other because they have different cultures. This may be because their cultures practice different religions or because they hold different **values**. Sometimes, different cultural groups fight one another in wars because their beliefs are conflicting, or opposing.

Even though people around the world are becoming more **tolerant** and accepting, these reasons for going to war may never completely disappear. This is because people are often motivated by, or make decisions based on, a want for power or the influences of their culture.

TYPES OF WAR

There are many different types of war. Many centuries ago, battles were often very similar—two armies would face each other and fight until one side **surrendered** or was completely killed. These battles were more likely to last for hours rather than years, and soldiers fought using horses and swords rather than tanks, bombs, and guns.

Wars have changed as technology has improved, meaning that wars can now be fought over many years, across large distances, and using many different kinds of weapons. Due to these changes, new types of wars have evolved. The different types of war are based on where the fighting takes place, who is fighting whom, and who has paid for the weapons, ammunition, and supplies.

CIVIL WARS

Civil wars are wars that are fought between two or more groups of people from the same country. They often involve a group in power of a country, such as the government, fighting against one or more rebel groups, made up of civilians. Civil wars occur for three main reasons:

TO TAKE CONTROL OVER AN ENTIRE COUNTRY

The English Civil War that took place between 1642 and 1651 is an example of this type of civil war. A group called the Roundheads wanted England to be controlled by a government, whereas an opposing group called the Royalists wanted the country to be controlled by a king or queen.

TO BECOME AN INDEPENDENT COUNTRY

The Second Sudanese War that took place between 1983 and 2005 involved a rebel group fighting the government to establish South Sudan as an **independent** country. South Sudan officially separated from Sudan in January 2005.

TO GET RID OF A GOVERNMENT

The Libyan Civil War that took place in 2011 is an example of this. Rebels fought to remove a **corrupt** leader and government. The war ended when the government was finally removed from power in October of 2011.

GUERRILLA WARS

Rather than gathering a large army together in one place, guerrilla wars use many small groups of soldiers who can more easily move around. Guerrilla warfare is often used in places where the **terrain** makes it difficult for large armies to move around, such as in jungles or on mountains. As they are not part of a larger army, guerilla soldiers sometimes fight using handmade weapons, such as bombs. They are sometimes local civilians, familiar with the land, who have a stake in the war of support the cause.

During guerrilla warfare, soldiers use the terrain to make it easier to attack large groups of enemies. One of the most common ways that this is done is through ambushes. An ambush is where a group hides, often in a jungle or on the side of a mountain. The group waits for its enemy to come close enough before launching a surprise attack. In successful ambushes, groups of only 10 or 20 people can easily defeat hundreds of enemies. Guerrilla armies are quick and mobile. They can attack and disappear in short order.

PROXY WARS

Proxy wars are wars where one side attempts to hurt their enemy by costing them money and attacking their **allies**, instead of attacking the enemy directly. Proxy wars usually start when two powerful countries are at war, but fighting each other directly would cause too much damage and cost too much money. So, one country might start fighting the other country's allies. This forces the country to support its allies and enter the war indirectly.

The Korean War memorial, in Washington, D.C., features statues of US soldiers. More than 36,000 American soldiers lost their lives during the war.

This was the case in the Korean War that took place between 1950 and 1953. At the time, the United States and the Soviet Union were involved in the Cold War. Instead of fighting each other directly, they fought each other through the Korean War. The United States sent soldiers, money, and weapons to South Korea, and the Soviets sent money, supplies and weapons to North Korea. The war cost both sides a lot of money. Many people believe that a lot more people would have died if the two powerful countries had fought each other directly.

CONSEQUENCES OF WAR

War affects people's families, homes, livelihoods, and survival. Its **consequences** are widespread. An immense number of soldiers and civilians have died in wars throughout history. Historians estimate that during World War II, the most deadly war in history, between 35 and 60 million people died. Since the start of the 20th century, with the development of more and more powerful weapons, it has been possible for wars to kill thousands of people in just one day.

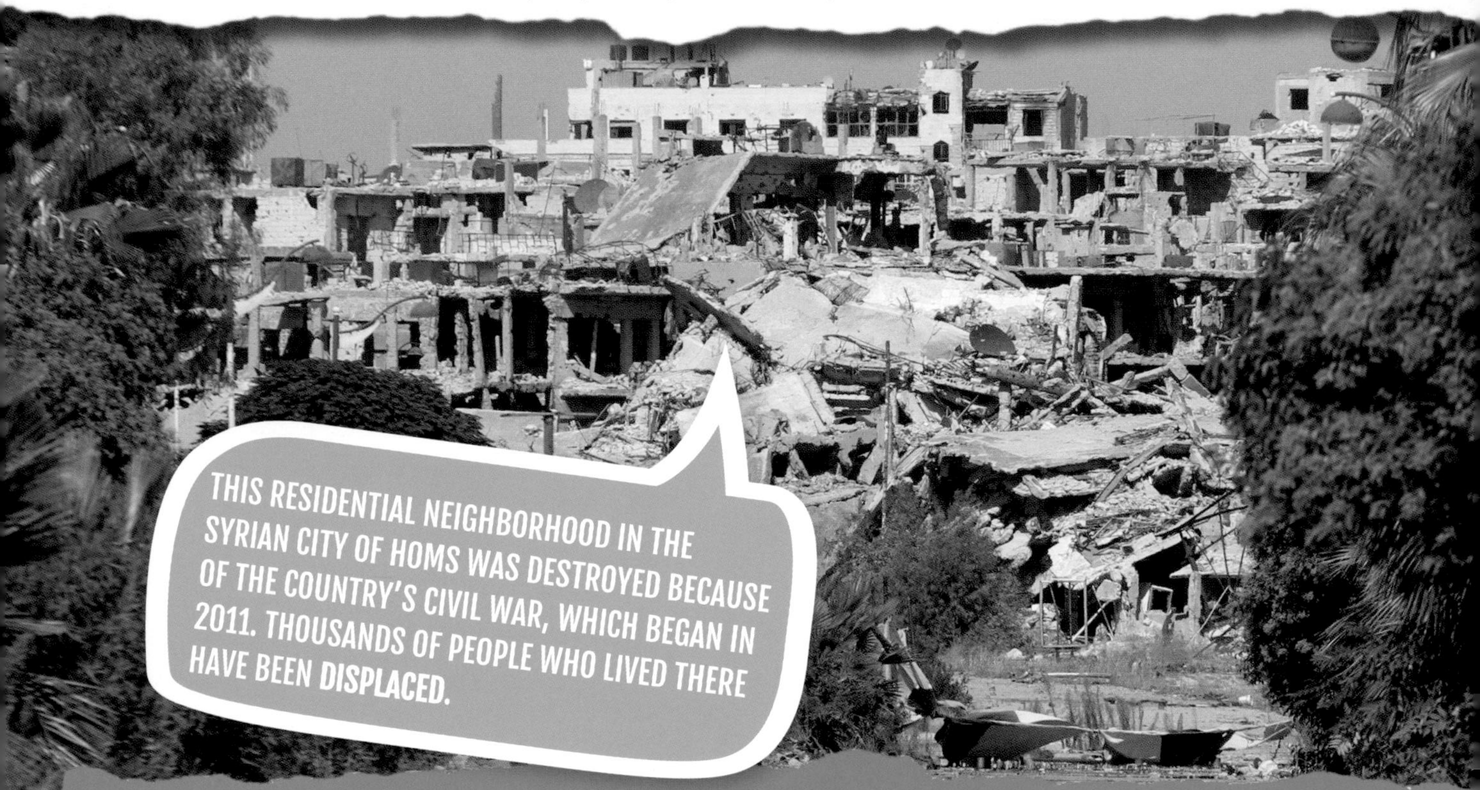

THIS RESIDENTIAL NEIGHBORHOOD IN THE SYRIAN CITY OF HOMS WAS DESTROYED BECAUSE OF THE COUNTRY'S CIVIL WAR, WHICH BEGAN IN 2011. THOUSANDS OF PEOPLE WHO LIVED THERE HAVE BEEN **DISPLACED.**

The consequences of war also greatly affect those who survive, as well as those who live in countries that are currently experiencing war. Many cities and towns are destroyed during wars, leaving people with no shelter. Families are often split apart during war, with parents and sometimes children being forced to become soldiers. Many children are unable to attend school. Wars also cost huge amounts of money. This means that fighting a long war can leave a country very poor. This can result countries being unable to rebuild homes and cities after a war ends. It can also cause a lack of food, services such as health care, and jobs for citizens, making it difficult to survive. Sometimes, survivors are unable to return to their homes after a war ends. A growing consequence of war, in recent years, has been the large number of refugees seeking help.

REFUGEES

Refugees are people who are forced to leave their country because they are not safe in their homes. Usually, their lives are in danger. Refugees often are unable to return to their homes, and are unsure whether they will be able to find a safe place to live in another country. Internally displaced persons, or IDPs, are people who are forced to leave their homes but remain in their country. They can face similar challenges to refugees.

The South Sudanese Civil War, which started in 2013, has forced nearly two million people to leave their homes in South Sudan and move to refugee camps in nearby countries, such as Uganda.

According to the United Nations High Commissioner for Refugees (UNHCR) in 2015, there were over 65 million people around the world who were forced from their homes. Sometimes, refugees are given **asylum** in other countries. Others are not as lucky. Many refugees and IDPs end up living in camps, because there is nowhere else for them to go. Refugee and IDP camps are usually crowded, with little space for housing and limited food, water, and medical care. They are often unsafe. Some refugees and IDPs are forced to live in camps for many years.

INTERNATIONAL LAWS

International laws are agreements between different countries. They are often related to **human rights**, the environment, and trading supplies and resources. International laws are often called "treaties" or "conventions." Many international laws are concerned with peace and war. For example, peace treaties are sometimes created when wars end. Peace treaties explain how the countries involved in a war will work together now that the war has ended.

THIS MAP SHOWS ALL OF THE COUNTRIES THAT ARE IN THE NORTH ATLANTIC TREATY ORGANIZATION (NATO). THE 28 COUNTRIES IN NATO HAVE ALL SIGNED A PEACE TREATY THAT SAYS THAT THEY WILL NOT FIGHT EACH OTHER AND THAT THEY WILL HELP PROTECT EACH OTHER IN ANY FUTURE WARS.

International laws are also made about what should be allowed in wars in the future, and how people are treated during wartime. During World War I, poisonous gases were used as a weapon by both sides. After the war, many people agreed that these gases weren't **humane**, because of the terrible effects they had on people. Because of this, the Geneva Protocol was made in 1928, which made it illegal under international law to use poisonous gas in armed conflicts.

HUMAN LIFE

Soldiers aren't the only people who lose their lives during a conflict. The civilians who live in **combat zones** are in extreme danger, too. Many have died in wars throughout history. Their homes are often destroyed through bombing or other fighting. If civilians survive these attacks, they have no where to go and are at risk of dying from starvation. Cities are bombed during wars for many different reasons. Sometimes it is because there are factories there that make weapons and other times it is because there are large army bases there. Whenever cities are bombed, many innocent civilians die.

In other wars, civilians are targeted and killed because of identifiers including their race, ethnicity, and religion. When a group targets and tries to kill people who are part of a certain race or religion, it is called **genocide**. During the Rwandan Civil War that took place in 1994, more than 800,000 Rwandan citizens were killed. They were mostly from the Tutsi ethnic group, and were targeted because of their ethnicity. This war is now known as the Rwandan genocide. Genocide is illegal in international law, according to the United Nation. Perpetrators of genocide are tried in the International Court of Justice for their crimes. However, it can take years for a case to make it to court and for a trial to be held.

SIGNIFICANT WARS IN HISTORY

AMERICAN WAR OF INDEPENDENCE

Before 1775, Britain had several **colonies** in North America, including a group of 13 in America. That year, the Thirteen Colonies rebelled against a series of laws, trade restrictions, and **taxes** they viewed as unfair. The colonies were forced to pay taxes to Britain but the colonists had no representation in British government. In 1776, the Thirteen Colonies declared independence as the United States of America. The rebellion and Declaration of Independence led to the American Revolutionary War (1775-83) and at its end, the beginning of a new country.

The Thirteen Colonies formed the Continental Congress, which was a meeting of delegates who formed a government during the Revolutionary War. In July, 1776, the Congress created and signed the Declaration of Independence, which explained how America would be governed once it won the war against the British.

Muskets took a long time to reload, so many muskets had bayonets on them in case the enemy got too close.

DATE: 1775 - 1783
DEATHS: AROUND 8,500 SOLDIERS
COUNTRIES INVOLVED: AMERICA AND BRITAIN
MAIN WEAPONS: MUSKETS, BAYONETS, AND CANNONS

AMERICAN WAR IN AFGHANISTAN

On the morning of September 11, 2001, two planes were **hijacked** and flown into the two towers of the World Trade Center in New York City. Two other planes were also hijacked. One crashed into the Pentagon, the U.S. Department of Defense headquarters, and another, headed toward Washington, D.C., crashed in a field in Pennsylvania. These attacks killed nearly 3,000 people and are known as the September 11 attacks.

These attacks were planned by a **terrorist group** called al-Qaeda, who were based in Afghanistan. Their leader at the time, Osama bin Laden, was already wanted by the American government and after the attacks they decided that the group had to be stopped from causing more damage and loss of life. Following the September 11 attacks, the United States declared war against Afghanistan.

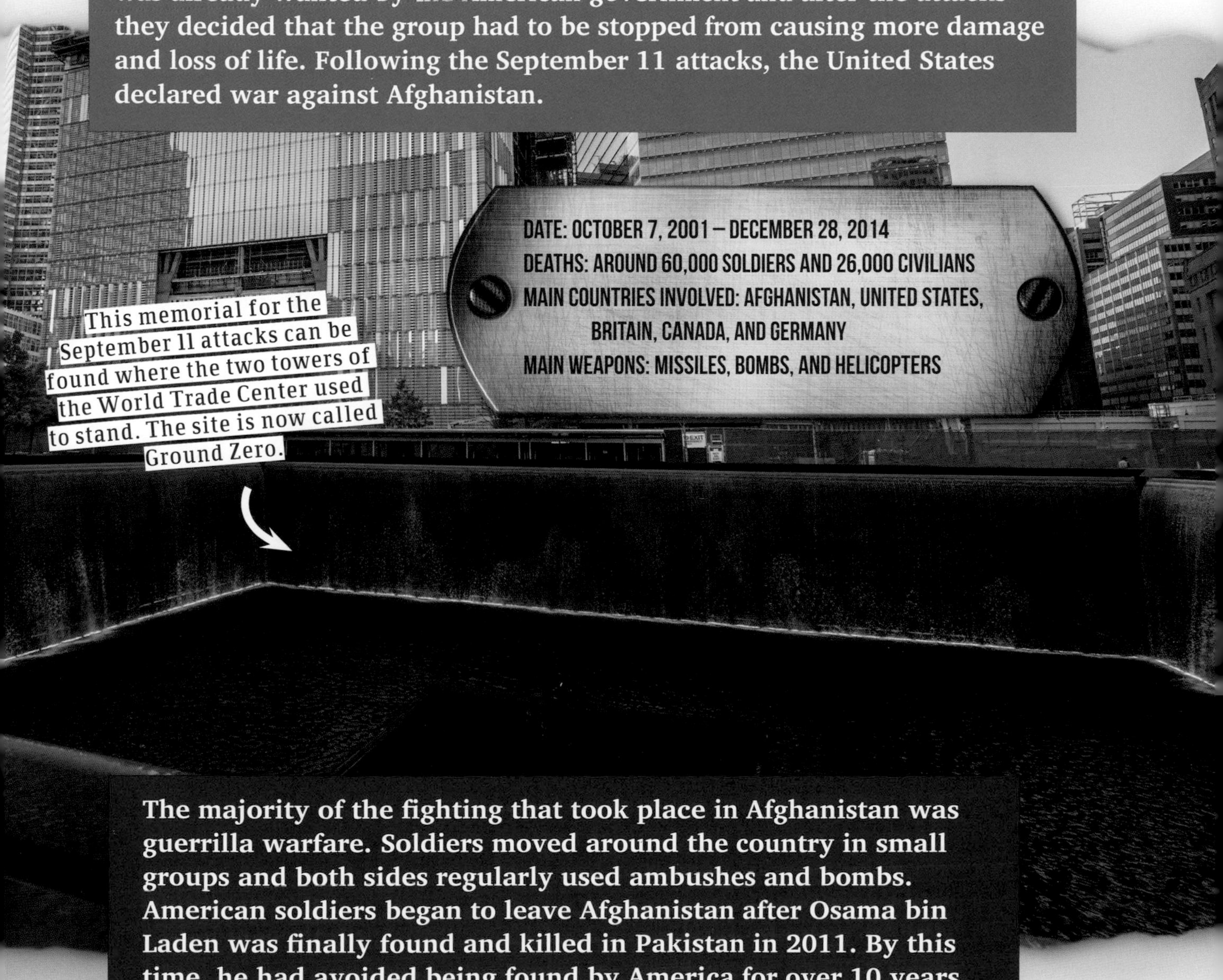

DATE: OCTOBER 7, 2001 – DECEMBER 28, 2014
DEATHS: AROUND 60,000 SOLDIERS AND 26,000 CIVILIANS
MAIN COUNTRIES INVOLVED: AFGHANISTAN, UNITED STATES, BRITAIN, CANADA, AND GERMANY
MAIN WEAPONS: MISSILES, BOMBS, AND HELICOPTERS

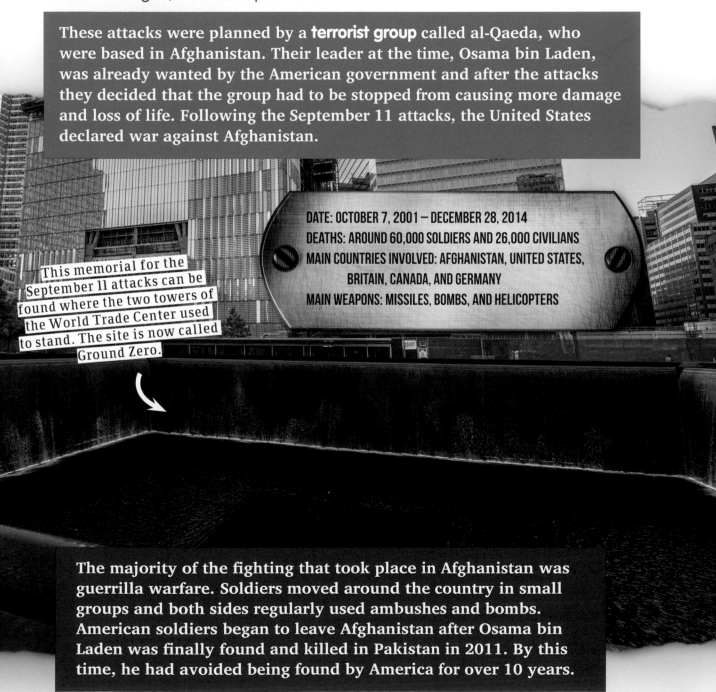

This memorial for the September 11 attacks can be found where the two towers of the World Trade Center used to stand. The site is now called Ground Zero.

The majority of the fighting that took place in Afghanistan was guerrilla warfare. Soldiers moved around the country in small groups and both sides regularly used ambushes and bombs. American soldiers began to leave Afghanistan after Osama bin Laden was finally found and killed in Pakistan in 2011. By this time, he had avoided being found by America for over 10 years.

WORLD WARS

WORLD WAR I

When World War I (WWI) started in 1914, it quickly became the biggest and most complicated war that the world had ever seen. The event that started the war was the **assassination** of the next king of **Austria-Hungary**, Archduke Franz Ferdinand, by a Serbian man named Gavrilo Princip. Believing that the Serbian government was behind the assassination, Austria-Hungary declared war on Serbia. After this, many of Serbia's and Austria-Hungary's allies joined the war.

SERBIA AND ITS ALLIES WERE CALLED THE ALLIED POWERS. AUSTRIA-HUNGARY AND ITS ALLIES WERE CALLED THE CENTRAL POWERS.

This map shows the countries that fought in WWI.

TRENCH WARFARE

WWI is known for its trench warfare. Trench warfare is a type of conflict where deep trenches are dug into the ground in order to protect soldiers from enemy bullets and **artillery**. Both sides used trench warfare during WWI, which made it very easy to defend your own ground but very difficult to take new ground from the enemy. For much of the war, no side managed to take any ground from the other, but hundreds of thousands of soldiers died trying.

CHEMICAL WARFARE

The other major type of warfare used in WWI was chemical warfare. At the time, chemical warfare had never been used in a war before. The trenches made it very difficult to attack the enemy using bullets or artillery, so both sides quickly started to use chemical warfare as it was able to reach the enemy in their trenches. Armies on both sides would send clouds of gas across no man's land, to reach opposing soldiers in their trenches.

DATE: JULY 28, 1914 – NOVEMBER 11, 1918
DEATHS: AROUND 10 MILLION SOLDIERS AND 7 MILLION CIVILIANS
MAIN ALLIED POWERS: FRANCE, ITALY, JAPAN, RUSSIA, UNITED STATES CANADA, AND BRITAIN
MAIN CENTRAL POWERS: AUSTRIA-HUNGARY, BULGARIA, AND GERMANY
MAIN WEAPONS: MACHINE GUNS, ARTILLERY, AND POISON GAS

A photograph taken of no man's land during WWI. No man's land is the space between two enemy trenches.

One of the worst chemicals used during WWI was chlorine gas, which burned people's eyes, mouth, throat, and lungs. Death from chlorine gas was very slow and painful and there was no way to treat it at the time. Other gases, such as **mustard gas**, were also used. Mustard gas was particularly harmful, as it attacked soldiers skin on contact—therefore bypassing protections such as gas masks. The use of chemical warfare was so inhumane that it was banned in international law, under the United Nations' Geneva Protocol in 1925. Despite this, chemical warfare is still sometimes used in war today.

WORLD WAR II

World War II (WWII) was even larger, more deadly, and more complicated than WWI. During the six years that WWII lasted, battles took place all over the world, from Pearl Harbor in Hawaii to Russia, Japan, and even countries in northern Africa. WWII started when Germany, led by Adolf Hitler, invaded Poland in 1939.

THE GERMAN WORD FOR LIGHTNING WAR IS BLITZKRIEG. THE BOMBINGS IN BRITAIN WERE CALLED THE "BLITZ" BECAUSE THE BOMBS CAME FROM THE SKY AND CAUSED A LOT OF DAMAGE, JUST LIKE LIGHTNING.

DATE: SEPTEMBER 1, 1939 – SEPTEMBER 2, 1945
DEATHS: AROUND 21 MILLION SOLDIERS AND 50 MILLION CIVILIANS
MAIN ALLIES: BRITAIN, UNITED STATES, SOVIET UNION (RUSSIA), FRANCE, CANADA, AND CHINA
MAIN AXIS POWERS: GERMANY, JAPAN, AND ITALY
MAIN WEAPONS: TANKS, MACHINE GUNS, AND BOMBS

Warfare in WWII often involved bombs, which both sides used in order to attack civilians and destroy cities. Between September 1940 and May 1941, cities in Britain were bombed over 100 times in attacks known as the "Blitz." In these eight months, over 40,000 British civilians were killed by bombs in their own cities. Many parents moved their children to the countryside in order to protect them from the bombs. These children, as well as other people who left the cities to escape the bombs, were called evacuees. At night, people had to black-out their windows and turn off all of the lights so that enemy pilots flying over Britain couldn't see where the cities were. Many cities in Britain, such as London, suffered extreme damage.

WWII ended when the U.S. dropped a new kind of bomb, called an **atomic bomb**, on two Japanese cities: Hiroshima and Nagasaki. The bombs were so powerful that these two bombings alone killed over 129,000 people, most of whom were civilians. Many people argue that the bombs should not have been dropped as they killed too many innocent people.

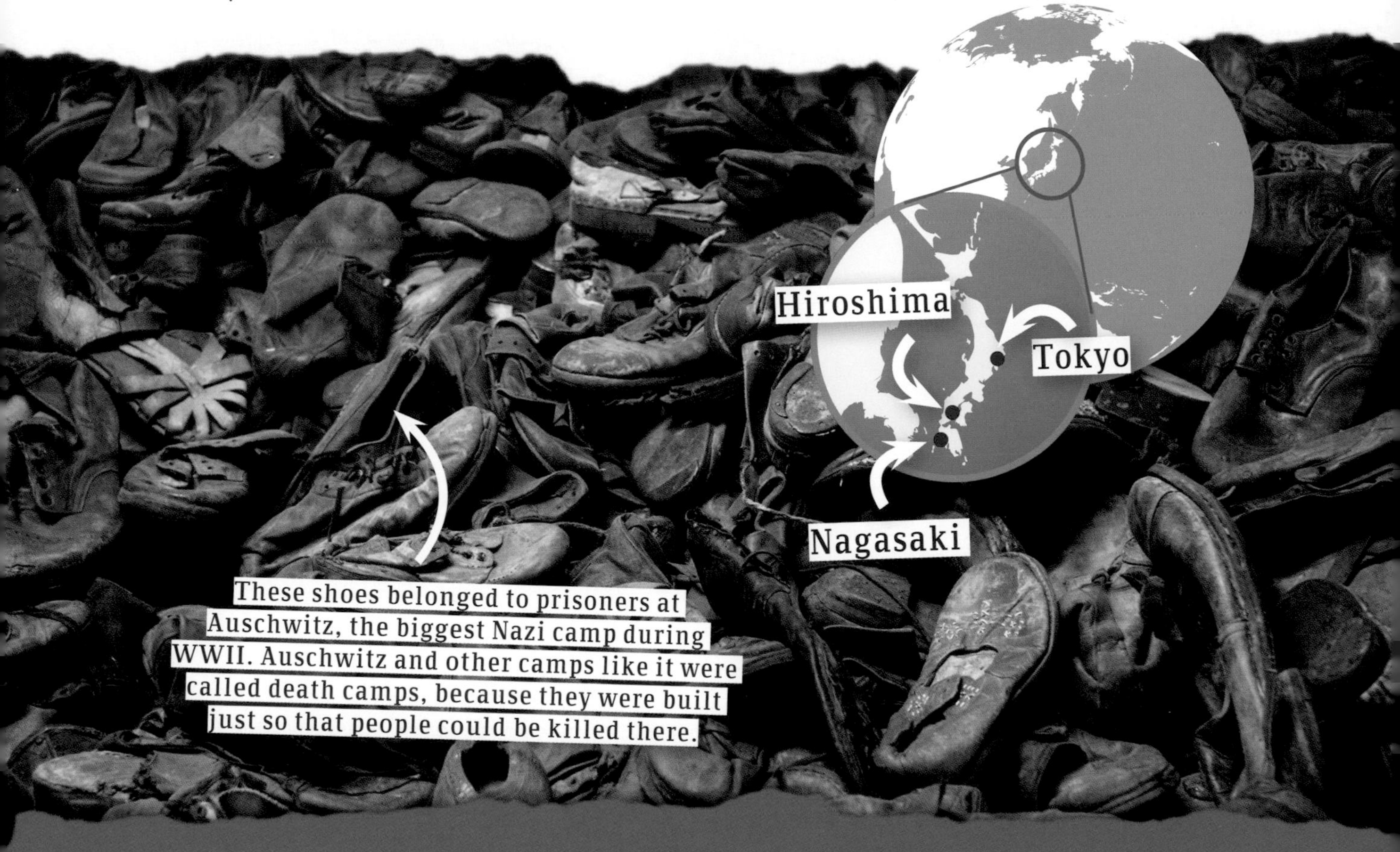

These shoes belonged to prisoners at Auschwitz, the biggest Nazi camp during WWII. Auschwitz and other camps like it were called death camps, because they were built just so that people could be killed there.

The most terrible event to occur during WWII was the Holocaust. The Holocaust was a genocide in which Adolf Hitler and his Nazi Party rounded-up and killed around six million Jewish people. The Nazis rounded up Jewish people in all of the countries that they invaded and sent them to camps. There, they were either forced to do work in terrible conditions or were immediately killed. Most of the people who died in these camps were killed by being sent into rooms that were filled with poisonous gas. As well as this, another 5 million other people were killed for reasons such as their race, political beliefs, sexuality, or if they were disabled. All of the people who died in the Holocaust were killed because the Nazis believed they were inferior. The Holocaust, and its victims, is remembered each year on International Holocaust Remembrance Day, January 27. It is widely considered to be the worst genocide in history.

MORALITY AND WAR

Wars have terrible consequences. Soldiers and civilians die, whole cities are destroyed, and people lose their homes, families, and livelihoods. War also means that governments and soldiers do terrible things to other humans. The events of war bring up questions of **morality**.

Some people accept the horrors of war, understanding that they need to occur in order for the war to be won and therefore end. Some argue that there are actions carried out within war that can never be **justified**, even if they would win a war. Others believe war is never right.

A white flag is a symbol of surrender. Most people agree that it is **immoral** to attack someone who is waving a white flag.

ACTIONS THAT MOST PEOPLE BELIEVE TO BE RIGHT OR GOOD ARE SAID TO BE "MORAL." ON THE OTHER HAND, ACTIONS THAT MOST PEOPLE BELIEVE TO BE WRONG OR BAD ARE CALLED "IMMORAL."

The morality of an action is how right or wrong that action is. The morality of an action isn't just based on the action itself. It looks at the **context** of the action, or the situation in which the action was performed. It also depends on the consequences of that action. For example, some people argue that although actions such as killing others or bombing cities are morally wrong, they can be justified during wartime if it means that an enemy will be stopped.

FORCE

A lot of people believe that it is immoral to use a large amount of force in a war. In this case, "force" means the number of soldiers, bullets, and bombs that are used to meet a goal, such as winning a battle or overtaking a city. Force is the amount of power used to attack an enemy. These people argue that the smallest amount of force possible should be used, so fewer people are affected and less damage is done.

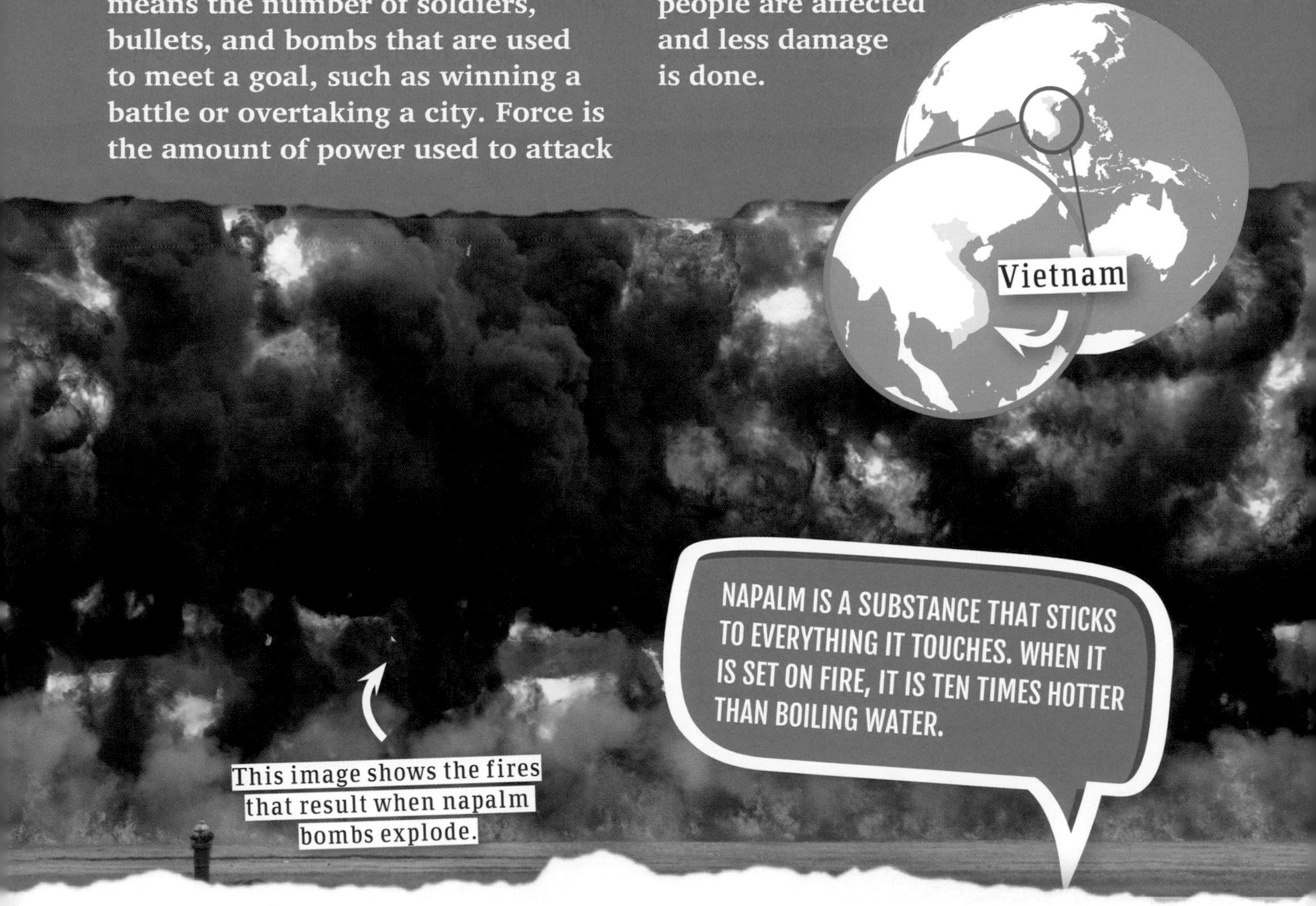

NAPALM IS A SUBSTANCE THAT STICKS TO EVERYTHING IT TOUCHES. WHEN IT IS SET ON FIRE, IT IS TEN TIMES HOTTER THAN BOILING WATER.

This image shows the fires that result when napalm bombs explode.

People's ideas of how moral or immoral a war is are often related to what kind of force was used during the war. Some tactics used by the American military in the Vietnam War, which took place in Vietnam and other nearby countries between 1955 and 1975, are considered immoral because of the type and level of force used. The United States and other anti-communist allies fought the Viet Cong, a communist group in South Vietnam, and the People's Army of Vietnam from communist North Vietnam. The Viet Cong used guerrilla warfare, hiding in villages in the jungles near American bases and inflicting quick and brutal damage. To attack the Viet Cong while they were hiding, the Americans used napalm, a liquid that catches fire. Some believe the use of napalm was immoral as it killed far more innocent people than Viet Cong soldiers.

CIVILIAN DEATH

Civilians are people who are not soldiers, who aren't helping their country to fight the war, and who might not have wanted their country to go to war in the first place. These people are innocent—but they are one of the most affected groups by warfare. Their homes, families, and lives are at risk. When thinking about the morality of war, people often ask if war is worth the killing of innocent people.

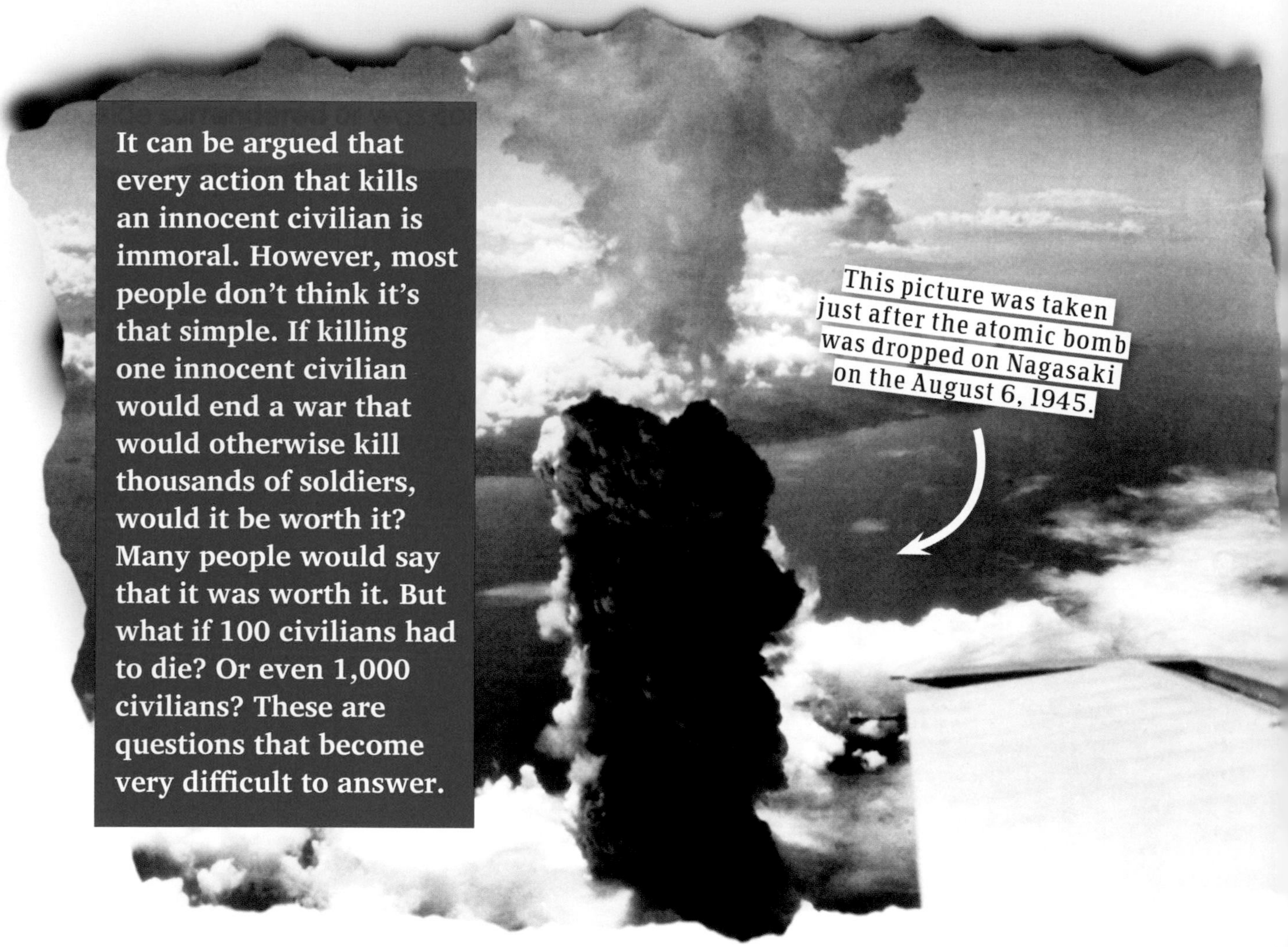

It can be argued that every action that kills an innocent civilian is immoral. However, most people don't think it's that simple. If killing one innocent civilian would end a war that would otherwise kill thousands of soldiers, would it be worth it? Many people would say that it was worth it. But what if 100 civilians had to die? Or even 1,000 civilians? These are questions that become very difficult to answer.

This picture was taken just after the atomic bomb was dropped on Nagasaki on the August 6, 1945.

The atomic bombs that the United States dropped on the Japanese cities of Hiroshima and Nagasaki ended WWII, but they also killed 129,000 people at once. Most of these people were civilians. The after-effects of the bombs were also devastating. **Radiation** caused by the bombs meant that many more people died of radiation sickness following the bombing, and survivors are still affected by illness today. While these bombs forced Japan to surrender, many people think that it was immoral to drop the bombs as they killed too many civilians. Others think the bombs ended the war earlier, thereby saving many more Allied lives.

LAST RESORT

The morality of a war doesn't just depend on what happens during the war. It can also relate to the reasons why the war started in the first place. Many people believe that the most immoral wars are the ones that were started for immoral reasons. For example, a war started for economic reasons, such as gaining access to a country's resources, might be considered immoral. The goal of this type of war is to make money from these resources. On the other hand, a war started to stop a country's dictator or oppressive government might be moral, as the goal of the war is to create a better life for the country's citizens.

It can be difficult to decide whether the reasons for a war are moral or immoral. There are many differing perspectives. Because of this, some people think that wars should always be a last resort. These people say that wars can only be moral when all other options have been tried first. This might include reaching a compromise with an enemy, or surrendering to avoid war.

PEACE AND WAR TODAY

As technology has changed and improved over time, the machines and weapons that are used in wars have become more powerful and deadly. Many armies around the world now had powerful artillery weapons, large air forces, many different types of bombs, strong naval forces, landmines, and countless guns. Although it is true that, since WWII, fewer soldiers die from war and the number of conflicts worldwide are decreasing, these machines and weapons make the world a more dangerous place for everyone.

It is believed that there are over 60,000,000 landmines left in the ground from previous wars in Africa and Asia. These are incredibly dangerous to the people who live in these areas. On top of this, there are around 15,000 nuclear weapons owned by different countries around the world today.

Many of these weapons are more powerful than the bombs that were dropped on Japan at the end of WWII. While the world may be becoming more peaceful, it is still full of very powerful weapons. There are various organizations that work toward stopping the use of these types of weapons.

ISRAEL AND PALESTINE

There are still many military conflicts going on around the world today. The longest-standing of these is the Israeli-Palestinian conflict, that has been going on for over 50 years.

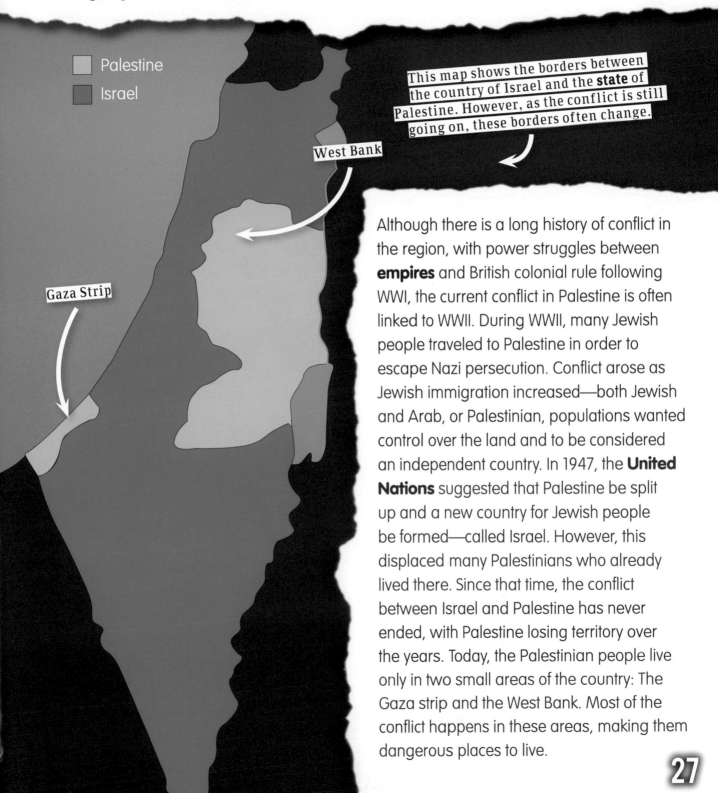

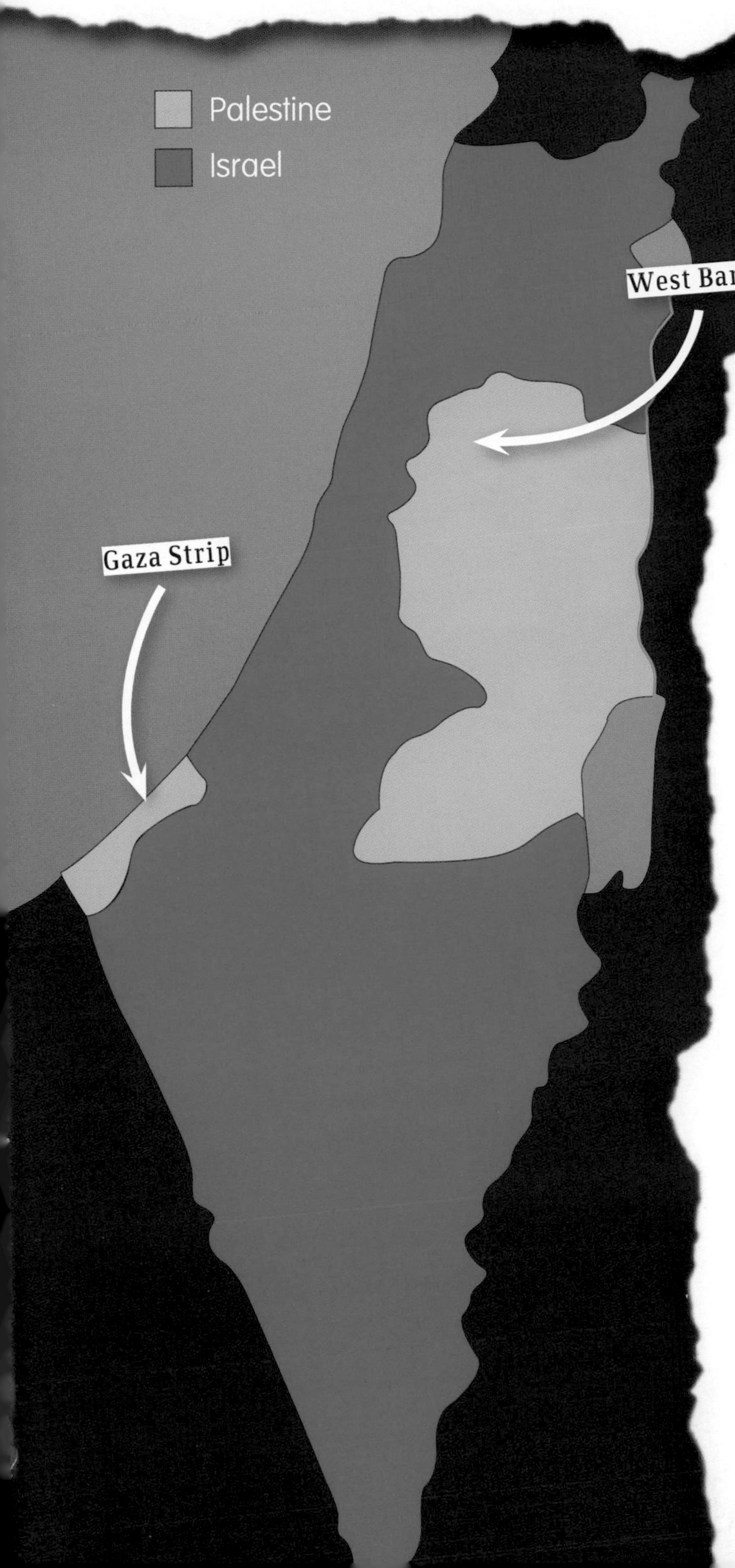

This map shows the borders between the country of Israel and the **state** of Palestine. However, as the conflict is still going on, these borders often change.

Although there is a long history of conflict in the region, with power struggles between **empires** and British colonial rule following WWI, the current conflict in Palestine is often linked to WWII. During WWII, many Jewish people traveled to Palestine in order to escape Nazi persecution. Conflict arose as Jewish immigration increased—both Jewish and Arab, or Palestinian, populations wanted control over the land and to be considered an independent country. In 1947, the **United Nations** suggested that Palestine be split up and a new country for Jewish people be formed—called Israel. However, this displaced many Palestinians who already lived there. Since that time, the conflict between Israel and Palestine has never ended, with Palestine losing territory over the years. Today, the Palestinian people live only in two small areas of the country: The Gaza strip and the West Bank. Most of the conflict happens in these areas, making them dangerous places to live.

SYRIA

Syria is currently one of the least peaceful countries on the planet. There has been a destructive civil war in the country for over five years.

The civil war began in 2011, between the Syrian people and the Syrian government. When some Syrian citizens began speaking out against the government in March 2011, the government responded with violent attacks against its own people. This resulted in rebel groups being formed to fight against the government's army. There were five major groups fighting in Syria in 2016. Each of these groups, as well as the Syrian government, had money and weapons sent to them by different countries around the world. These countries include the United States, Russia, Turkey, Saudi Arabia, and Iran. Because so many other countries are involved in the war, backing it and providing assistance, many people view it as a proxy war.

This is the Arch of Triumph in Palmyra, Syria. It was built by the Romans over 1,500 years ago. In 2015, the Arch of Triumph was destroyed as a result of the war in Syria.

Since the start of the war, over half of the country's population has either been killed or forced to leave their homes. Over four million Syrians have become refugees, hundreds of thousands of soldiers and civilians have been killed, and many important historical sites have been destroyed. An estimated 13.5 million Syrians needed humanitarian assistance because of the war.

Although wars are still being fought around the world, peace is still possible. While there are some places such as Syria, South Sudan, and Palestine, that have become less peaceful in the last few years, many states and territories around the world have become more peaceful. More children are now able to go to school. More people now have the human rights they deserve. More people are tolerant of different cultures, religions, and races. And more and more people now have the freedom to live their lives as they wish.

There are also lots of organizations around the world, such as humanitarian aid groups like the International Rescue Committee (IRC), that work to promote and preserve peace, improve human rights, and make sure that people have the supplies and resources that they need to survive. It is important to learn about the current wars and conflicts affecting people around the world today, and learn how we can help. Organizations that work to promote peace and human rights can give us the information we need about people in need, and how we can help. There is still a long way to go—but peace may be in our world's future.

CLASS DISCUSSIONS

What do you think is the worst consequence of war? Discuss your thoughts.
In your opinion, what is most important when trying to ensure that a war is moral?
Take a look at the images and captions below to help get you thinking.

Not using too much force.

Making sure that civilians are not hurt.

Making sure that it is a last resort.

Search online to find an organization that works to promote peace, support human rights, or offer humanitarian aid. Share this organization with a classmate. What is one way you could help support this organization?

GLOSSARY

allies	Countries that work together, often for military reasons
ammunition	Bullets, shells, missiles, and bombs
arms	Part of the army; to carry weapons
artillery	Very large guns used in warfare on land
assassination	The killing of an important person, usually for political or religious reasons
asylum	Protection given by a country to someone who has fled their home
atomic bomb	A destructive type of nuclear weapon that explodes because of the release of atomic energy
Austria-Hungary	An empire made up of the lands owned by Austria and Hungary that existed from 1867 to 1918
civilians	People not in the army or police force
colonies	Areas under the control of another country and occupied by people from that country
combat zones	The area where fighting during war takes place
commemorate	To remind or be a memorial of
conflict	A serious disagreement or fight
context	The conditions in which something exists
consequences	The results or effects of an action or actions
corrupt	To be dishonest or unethical for personal gain
culture	The traditions, ideas, and ways of life of a particular group of people
displaced	To force someone to leave their home
empires	A large group of states or countries under the rule of a single leader or government
genocide	The deliberate or targeted killing of a specific group of people, meant to exterminate or completely get rid of their population
governments	Groups of people with the authority to run countries and decide their laws
hijacked	To have taken control of a vehicle or machine illegally
human rights	Rights that every person should have
humane	Showing kindness and a respect for life
independent	Free from outside control
inferior	Lower in status
issues	Important topics or problems
justified	Done for a good reason
landmines	Bombs laid on or just under the ground
military	A country's army and the things that relate to it
morality	A system of thoughts and actions related to what is believed to be right and wrong
mustard gas	A type of chemical weapon that affects skin and lungs
naval	Relating to a navy, which is the part of an army that operates at sea
nuclear weapons	Very destructive weapons that use nuclear energy
race	A group of people who have similar physical characteristics, coming from a common ancestry
radiation	A form of energy that comes from a nuclear reaction that can be harmful it comes in contact with humans
surrendered	Stopped fighting the enemy and accepted that the enemy had won
sustainable	Able to be maintained or kept for a long time
tactics	Carefully planned actions and strategies in a war
taxes	Payments made to the government so that they can provide services to citizens
terrain	The physical features of land
terrorist group	People who cause damage and death in order to scare and intimidate governments and civilians
tolerant	Able to accept beliefs, opinions, and behaviors that you disagree with
tranquillity	The state of being calm and free from disturbance
United Nations	An international organization created in 1945 to promote peace and cooperation between countries
values	Standards of behavior and beliefs on what is important in life

INDEX